Fruit of the Spirit

By Dana Poole

Kamikaze for Christ

To live is Christ; to die is gain.

Philippians 1:21

All Rights Reserved

Unless otherwise indicated, Scripture quotations are taken from the

King James Bible version of the Bible

Kamikaze for Christ Ministries

A Ministry of *Lost Sheep Ministries*

©2011 By Dana Poole

What is a *Kamikaze* for Christ?

The correct definition of the word *Kamikaze* is translated to *mean divine wind from the legendary name of a typhoon that in 1281 saved Japan by destroying the Mongol navy)* : kami, **divine** + kaze, **wind.** God lay upon my heart that there is no other divine wind like the presence of our living God working through His people by the power of the Holy Spirit. As it is stated in Philippians 1:21- To live is Christ....to die is gain. Just as that divine wind saved Japan from their enemy so can we be that in our own lives and the lives of others. A kamikaze for Christ is defined as an individual who is willing to invade the enemy's camp and defeat him with no regard to self. Their life is laid down with a reckless abandon for the cause of Christ, All for His Glory. All for His purpose, Yielded to the Holy Ghost, full of the Word of God, diligent, watchful, and always wielding a ready sword.

A word from Pastor Bob Gibson
President and Founder of *Lost Sheep Ministries*

Dana is a godly woman who walks in great humility and integrity. She honors the Lord with her daily devotion to Him in every area of life. Her knowledge of the Word and her love for people is expressed in all she does. Dana's sensitivity to the Holy Spirit would make her an excellent candidate wherever she would minister. I highly recommend her. Dana is a wonderful speaker with a warm personality who also knows the Word very well and how to apply it. She operates very strongly in the prophetic with incredible precision and timing. You will be greatly blessed to have her speak at your next event.

Pastor Bob Gibson

Until He comes......
We will go

Dana is a speaker, teacher and minister available for retreats and seminars.
Contact her via email at poolend1@gmail.com or via phone 281.650.9932

Table of Contents

But the fruit of the Spirit is *love, joy, peace, longsuffering, gentleness, goodness, faith, Meekness, temperance*: against such there is no law. And they that are Christ's <u>have</u> crucified the flesh with the affections and lusts. If we live in the Spirit, let us also walk in the Spirit.

Galatians 5:22-25 (KJV)

Fruit of the Spirit

Galatians 5:22-25 (King James Version)

> But the fruit of the Spirit is *love, joy, peace, longsuffering, gentleness, goodness, faith, Meekness, temperance*: against such there is no law. And they that are Christ's _have_ crucified the flesh with the affections and lusts. If we live in the Spirit, let us also walk in the Spirit.

In this Bible study we will focus on the Spirit's part more or as much as we will focus on the fruit, for it is by the Spirit of God in us that we bear the fruit . God has given me a different perspective on this subject. I am very careful not to say that it is new because God says there is nothing new under the sun (Ecc. 1:9) and I am sure I am not the only one that God has revealed this to. I think you will find as we go along that the Holy Spirit has been revealing these things to you as well. Our ultimate goal by the end of this study is to have a walk that is so controlled by the Holy Spirit that we are amazed at the fruit we bear.

We will study each fruit individually. There will be home work, Scripture memorization and a time of personal inventory. We are going to let the Word of God change the way we think about the fruit of the Spirit by renewing our minds and yielding to THE Spirit.

The first thing I want you to do is throw out the old saying-"Don't pray for patience cause God will give you trials so that you will *learn* patience" God simply asked me this question one day," Dana , why are you asking for what you already have?" At that point my whole way of looking at the fruit changed. It was like someone took my head in their hands and turned it just slightly and said, "Look over here just a little to the right and you will see what you need to see". I began to understand what God was telling me. He never intended on us *learning* to bear fruit. He desires us to learn to *yield* to the Holy Spirit so the fruit of the Spirit can come forth. I was sharing this with my husband Nathan, and he said to me this:" Does an apple tree have to learn to bear apples?" We already have ALL the fruit of the Spirit because we are born again believers.

Let's look up the following verses and confirm this with the Word:

Ezekiel 36:27
John 14:17
Romans 8:9
1 Corinthians 3:16
2 Corinthians 4:7
2 Timothy 1:14
1 John 2:20, 24-27

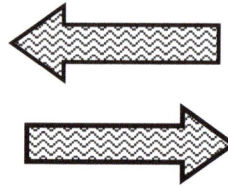

Now that we have confirmed that we are indeed filled with the Spirit then the question arises, why is it so hard to bear all those wonderful fruits that are the character of Christ? The problem is not in our learning. It is not in how we pray or anything to do with what we are able to do at all. It has to do with us recognizing that the Holy Spirit in us *is* or *should* be the one in charge or in control. Are we yielding that authority to Him? Are we letting Him rule our mind, will and emotions? Read this section from my Journal: ....

I do recognize that Your Holy Spirit is the ruling authority in my life. My opinions are not right unless they line up with Your Word. My feelings and emotions are all liars. My flesh is selfish and corrupted by its own lusts. All I have that is good, is You. I subject myself to Your Holy Spirit today. Consume me with Your character. Cause me to be lead by You alone. Tune me into Your voice that I am able to hear and do Your will. Make me a blessing to someone today.

This is a choice that must be made, every day, every hour, every moment. We cannot bear the precious fruit on our own, but hallelujah we can by yielding over control, authority and leadership to the Holy Spirit that lives in us. This is not something that can be taught by just merely giving information. This is Christian principle that we must learn to implement into our daily lives. When we study each fruit and learn what the Word has to say about it, then we will discuss how and where we must yield in order to bear that fruit in our lives. We will learn where we have not yet given that control over to the Holy Spirit. We will also learn that by yielding authority and control over to the Holy Spirit we are guarded from the enemy. Hallelujah!!

Why are we learning this? As Kamikaze's for Christ, we want to be fruit bearers. We want all who we minister to, all we fellowship with, to see the fruit we bear that Glorifies God; that causes others to want what we have. We will become so yielded to Him that we are untouchable and unstoppable by the enemy. Ladies, it is time for us to be busy about the Father's work. As His handmaidens we have a calling, and a purpose that is great. The key to stepping into it is letting Him be the boss. Are you ready? Ok, your homework is to take your write out the memory Verse and put it in a place where you will read it every day at least once. Meditate on it and begin now asking the Lord to give you revelation on the areas where you are still in control and you need to yield over to Him. Ask Him to make real to you that you are filled with the Holy Spirit and begin speaking to the Spirit of God, acknowledging His presence in your life. Write out your prayer that you will pray every day (refer to my journal entry) Ask Him to help you yield and then proclaim to yourself and your flesh that you *will* yield!

Your Memory Verse is Galatians 5:22-25

My Prayer:

_____

_____

_____

_____

_____

_____

_____

_____

_____

_____

_____

_____

_____

_____

_____

_____

_____

My area to work on:

_____

_____

_____

_____

_____

_____

_____

_____

My favorite "filled with the Holy Spirit" Verse from the list:

(Write it here once a day for 5 days)

_____

_____

_____

_____

_____

_____

_____

_____

_____

_____

_____

_____

_____

_____

_____

My Personal Notes as I Mediate on Galatians 5: 22-25:

_____

_____

_____

_____

_____

_____

_____

_____

_____

_____

_____

_____

_____

_____

_____

_____

_____

_____

_____

_____

_____

_____

_____

_____

_____

LOVE

The first thought that comes to my mind concerning LOVE is how hard it is to do at times. Love is an action word. It is something that we do not merely say. Like all the other fruit of the Spirit it is something that is produced in and through us by our submission and yielding to the Holy Spirit. We, in our flesh, in our human nature, can never produce the type of love that is referred to here. It is direct evidence that the Holy Spirit of God rules and reigns in our life. Just as apples are direct evidence that a tree is indeed an apple tree. Oh how I want to be a love tree to represent Jesus in this world!

The next place my mind goes concerning the fruit of love is pride and how it is what trips us up most of the time; keeping us from bearing that precious fruit of love. Humility, being the opposite of pride of course, is our key, our way of escape from the temptation or snare of pride (1 Corn. 10:13). Let's lay our foundation for submission and humility by reading the Word of God. These Verses bring it all into perspective. We are no better or worse than the person sitting next to us. We are all the same in the eyes of God. His love is the same for each of us because it all hinges on our faith in Jesus Christ, not by our works (Eph. 2:9) Therefore in the following list of Scriptures we see how He desires us to position ourselves in love. We position ourselves by making the choice to yield our rights, opinions, comforts, desires, thoughts, will and emotions over to the Holy Spirit, in order that love may come forth. Read the following Verses:

Romans 5:5
Romans 12:9-10
Phil 2:1-5
Eph. 4:1-6

In these verses the common thread screams, *"Love brings the unity and peace that is needed for the body of Christ to work. Get over yourselves, get over the pettiness and love each other all ready with the love I have shed abroad in your heart."* Hallelujah! Say, "It's not about me!"

We best represent Him when His love is flowing freely through us to a lost and dying world. Loving the unlovable is a wonderful opportunity to show forth the precious fruit of love. Loving our enemies or those who persecute us is an example of the love of Christ. Remember what the Word says about that- *"But God commendeth his love toward us, in that, while we were yet sinners, Christ died for us."* Romans 5:8. Jesus did not wait until we were lovable to lay His life down for us. Thank You Jesus!

Read the following verses:

Matthew 5:44
Luke 6:27
Luke 6:35

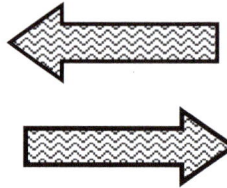

The last one there in Luke speaks to my heart because that is where He tells us we shall be children of the Highest. Oh how that excites me! I spent so much time effort and energy being a child of the devil; serving self and promoting unrighteousness. The very concept that I can be a representative of HIS great LOVE is overwhelming to say the least. Is it hard? YES! But He also tells us our reward will be great. Jesus knows that it goes against our carnal nature. He understands that we will battle this. In fact He tells us in Hebrews 4:15 *"For we have not an high priest which cannot be touched with the feeling of our infirmities; but was in all points tempted like as we are, yet without sin."* He gets it! That is why we must yield over control to the Holy Spirit; our human nature cannot love that way. No matter how hard you try, you cannot *learn* to love like Jesus. It MUST be Him loving them *through* you by way of the Holy Spirit. Well I just made that sound so simple didn't I! I have not yet hit on the things that get in our way of yielding to the Spirit so we can love. Here is what God has given me on this.

We must do away with the following things and thought patterns:

Critical thinking that puts down a person instead of edifying them
My opinion is right. My way is right
Arrogance and pride in one's self or accomplishments
Thinking that we are better than someone else
Judging another by their sin or weakness
OUR RIGHTS!
Self-Centered thinking that keeps us from being sensitive to another's needs
Bitterness
Unforgiveness

This list is not all inclusive of everything, but it is a start. I trust God will reveal your hindrances. I know if you seek Him and truly ask Him to reveal them to you, He will.

Look at this word and its meaning: <u>Deference</u>—a yielding of judgment or preference from respect to the wishes or opinion of another; submission in opinion; regard; respect. Deference marks an inclination to yield one's opinion in the sentiments of another in preference to one's own. We need to be more deferent towards others.

Say this with me:

"Everything is not always about me or my wants or my needs or my preferences, what I have to say or what I think!"

Refer to Philippians 2: 3-4

³Let nothing be done through strife or vainglory; but in lowliness of mind let each esteem other better than themselves. ⁴Look not every man on his own things, but every man also on the things of others.

God continually directs us in His Word to put others first before ourselves and the things of the Kingdom before the things of the world.

He wants us to know the kind of love He felt when He was hanging on the cross and He said, *"Father forgive them for they know not what they do."* Luke 23:34. The love that must have been flooding His heart at that moment was the strength that kept Him in His Father's will to stay upon the cross. It says in Hebrews 12:2 *looking unto Jesus the author and finisher of our faith;* **who for the joy that was set before him endured the cross,** *despising the shame, and is set down at the right hand of the throne of God.* I believe that joy was our salvation! Let us also be quick to remember that LOVE is something that is done. Real love will demand action from us, for mere words is just not enough to satisfy. Love has power it says in 1 Peter 4:8 *"Above all things have fervent charity (love) among yourselves; for charity (love) shall cover the multitude of sins."* Now that is powerful love! Love is power. It moves the heart and it reaches in the depths of our being in places where nothing else can seem to go. This is the *agape* love that is from God, not human love. This same love, this same power can flow through us to our families, loved ones and the world if only we yield to the Holy Spirit. As we pursue to yield to the Holy Spirit may we also keep close to our hearts and minds that we do not know who may be watching us as we love the unlovable and as we walk in love with fellow believers. Our example of love could win many to Christ! Hallelujah, how Heaven rejoices when one is born again!

Homework:_   **Meditate on Romans 5:5**

What are my problem areas where I am not being deferent towards others and/or
yielding myself to the Holy Spirit so the precious fruit of Love can come forth in my life?
Ask the Lord to show you. Write them down here.

_____

_____

_____

_____

_____

_____

_____

_____

_____

_____

Now take those things, habits, or thought patterns and write out a prayer to God giving
those areas over to Him and declaring that you are yielding them over to the Holy Spirit.

_____

_____

_____

_____

_____

_____

_____

_____

_____

_____

_____

_____

_____

_____

_____

Find 5 more Scriptures in your Bible that refer to love in a way that is special to you or speaks to your heart. Write them out here. Be ready to share with the group.

_____

_____

_____

_____

_____

_____

_____

_____

_____

_____

_____

_____

_____

_____

_____

_____

_____

_____

What is your favorite "LOVE" Scripture? Write it once a day for 5 days.

_____

_____

_____

_____

_____

_____

_____

_____

_____

_____

_____

_____

_____

_____

_____

_____

_____

_____

_____

_____

_____

_____

How I applied the yielding principle this week to bear the fruit of love.

_____

_____

_____

_____

_____

My Personal Notes as I meditate on Romans 5:5

_____

_____

_____

_____

_____

_____

_____

_____

_____

_____

_____

_____

_____

_____

_____

_____

_____

JUST OBEY YIELD

When there is an absence of JOY in our lives it manifests in many ways. We are tired and sometimes apathetic. Everything seems so hard. Getting through each day is a push. To accomplish what is necessary seems pointless and appears to have no real purpose. Life is empty; depression, apathy and self-pity lurk very close just waiting for its opportunity to have an effect on you. I have truly sought the Lord on this and once again He so graciously sets me straight. We have been taught that we lose our joy but I present to you another perspective. We have all the joy that the Holy Spirit can possibly possess; because we have the Holy Spirit. We must yield in order for that fruit to manifest in our lives. The absence of joy reveals that there is a problem with our obedience and yielding. JUST OBEY and YIELD. It is not complicated or confusing as the enemy would have us to think. It is not contingent on our circumstances or emotions, Hallelujah! The fruit of joy is revealed in us when we are yielded to Him in such a way that the truth of His Word lightens our hearts, our eternity with Him excites us, and our faith in His sovereign power gives us strength. Let's look at the Scriptures concerning joy.

Nehemiah 8:10
Romans 14:17
1Peter 1:8-9
Psalm 51:12
Psalm 5:11
Acts 20:24
Isaiah 12:3
Psalm 16:1
Psalm 35:9
John 15:11

I've got the JOY, JOY, JOY, JOY
Down in My Heart.............

One of the primary ways that we hinder the fruit of joy in our lives is where we put our focus. Are we focused on the affairs of this life or on the eternal things of God? Are we focused on what the world tells us or what the Word of God tells us? Let's look at Romans 14:17 *for the kingdom of God is not meat and drink; but righteousness, and peace, and joy in the Holy Ghost.* This verse is turning my focus from the issues of this natural life, even its needs; to KINGDOM attributes and then tells me that righteousness, peace and joy are all available to me in the Holy Ghost. Hallelujah! Do I mean to tell you that all you have to do is change your focus and realize that the joy you need is already in you by way of the Holy Spirit? YES!! However, we must consider then the reason we do not have this joy is our own doing. If we are anxious, not trusting Him, not being obedient to what He has told us to do or NOT to do then we block that joy.

The joy of the Lord is strength. It comes from the Holy Spirit yet it quickens our flesh and gives us strength to do His will. The joy of the Lord attracts others, more so than any of the other fruit due to the strength that is felt from being around that joy. Have you ever been around someone with that joy and felt better, stronger in their presence? That is the fruit of joy at work. Happiness won't do that for others around you because it is merely an emotion, however the fruit of joy brings strength to all it comes into contact with. We should be quick to remember that the fruit we bear is not only for us but it is for others to partake of and to be blessed by it. Just like when you eat an apple from an apple tree. Yes, the tree benefits from the seeds that the apple produces, but the people who eat the apples are nourished by it and they enjoy its sweetness. You want to bring others to Christ? You want your family to be saved? Then **J**ust **O**bey and **Y**ield. Cast off the lies of the enemy that will tell you it's not that simple. You will find that the search for where you are hindering the fruit of Joy will begin in the Word of God. His Word is your mirror. God will use the Scriptures to show you where you are not obeying Him and yielding to Him. I will ask you this," Are you ready to be real with yourself and real with God?" You must fight for your Joy! You must fight <u>lies</u> from the enemy. You must fight your own <u>emotions</u>. You must fight your <u>flesh</u>. Not one of those 3 has the power to defeat you unless you let it.

On the next page there is a list of areas that hinder or block the fruit of joy. Prayerfully consider each topic and write a brief description of how it would stop the fruit of joy. Then look at the Scriptures I have provided and match it up with the appropriate topic and write out the verse in the space provided.

Worry   Scripture_____

_____   _____

_____   _____

_____   _____

_____   _____

Procrastination   Scripture_____

_____   _____

_____   _____

_____   _____

_____   _____

Anger   Scripture_____

_____   _____

_____   _____

_____   _____

_____   _____

Money/Bills   Scripture_____

_____   _____

_____   _____

_____   _____

_____   _____

Relationships   Scripture_____

_____   _____

_____   _____

_____   _____

_____   _____

Complaining

_____
_____
_____
_____
_____

Scripture_____

_____
_____
_____
_____

Not reading the Bible

_____
_____
_____
_____
_____

Scripture_____

_____
_____
_____
_____

Not spending time in prayer

_____
_____
_____
_____
_____

Scripture_____

_____
_____
_____
_____

Selfishness

_____
_____
_____

Scripture_____

_____
_____
_____

Phil 4:6-7	Matthew 26:36	Mark 10:37	Deuteronomy 6:4-9
Ephesians 4:26-27	Matthew 26:41	Acts 24:25	Psalm 1:1-6
Matthew 6:19-20	Ephesians 4:29	Matthew 8:21	Amos 3:3
Malachi 3:10-12	Phil 2:14-15	Luke 9:61	Matthew 12 :28-30
2 Timothy 2:15	Proverbs 11:26	Genesis 19:16	Phil 4:11-12
Mark 6:46	Isaiah 5:8	2 Corinthians 6:14	Phil 4:19
Matthew 14:23	Matthew 25:43	Ephesians 5:11	Colossians 3:8

From the list of Scriptures on the first page of this lesson, which one is your favorite? Which one speaks to you? Write it here every day for 5 days.

_____

_____

_____

_____

_____

_____

_____

_____

_____

_____

_____

_____

_____

_____

_____

_____

_____

_____

_____

_____

_____

_____

_____

_____

_____

Prayerfully ask the Lord what are your personal areas where you need the fruit of joy to come forth.

_____

_____

_____

_____

_____

_____

_____

_____

_____

Read John 15:11: **Meditate on this verse this week**

What was Jesus referring to when He said- "These things have I spoken unto you?"
And what does that mean to you concerning "joy" being in your life?

_____

_____

_____

_____

_____

_____

_____

_____

_____

_____

_____

After reflecting on the Scriptures and this lesson, what will you ask yourself from now on when you find an absence of joy in your life?

_____

_____

_____

_____

_____

_____

_____

In the LOVE lesson we talked about a yielding principle, how is the yielding principle different in the JOY lesson?

_____

_____

_____

_____

_____

_____

_____

_____

_____

_____

_____

_____

Peace

Peace, what does it really mean? We all seek it, crave it, and at times are desperate for it. Peace in the Biblical sense is a state of total well-being, inner harmony between God and man. The first place we must seek peace is between us and God. If we know we are not living right, doing what He has asked us to do or in rebellion towards God, we will not have peace in our lives in any way, inward or outward. The sweet fruit of peace will be far from our reach until we make our peace with God and only you and Him know what the issue is that needs to be yielded over.

I asked the Lord this question, "What is our greatest hindrance from having the fruit of peace flowing freely from our lives?" As I searched the Scriptures God began to speak to my heart. I saw that trusting Him was our biggest obstacle. We pray, spend time in His Word, even share Christ with others.....BUT we have trouble trusting Him in our own lives or in the lives of those dearest to our heart. Trust is mandatory in order to have real peace, true peace. Read the following Scriptures:

Philippians 4:6-7
Isaiah 26:3,4
Colossians 3:15
Romans 12:18
Psalm 34:14
James 3:18
Hebrews 12:14
Romans 5:1
John 14:27
Psalm 29:11

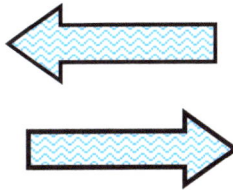

I have the Peace that passes understanding Down in my Heart...............

YOU MUST HAVE READ THE PREVIOUS SCRIPTURES BEFORE READING THIS PAGE

Consider this:

Philippians 4:6-7; Tells us not to worry. To pray and leave it with Him and HIS peace will **KEEP** our hearts and minds. He is telling us to *trust* Him.

Isaiah 26:3,4; His peace will **KEEP** us and **STRENGTHEN** us because we *trust* Him.

Colossians 3:15; Let (which means to give permission or allow) His peace to **RULE** our hearts. We cannot give permission to or allow, unless we first *trust.*

Do you see the common thread in these Scriptures? We cannot have the peace that passes all understanding if we do not trust the one who we are asking to grant us that peace. Also I ask you to consider this fact; Peace is a fruit of the Holy Spirit, which we have previously determined that we already have, so do we need to ask for it? I believe what God is showing us through His Word is if we truly *TRUST* him then the fruit of peace is loosed in us and will flow freely. The issue we must search out for ourselves and ask God to reveal to us is this: <u>Where do we not trust Him?</u> When He shows us then we must *repent* from not trusting him in these areas. Ask His forgiveness, let Him wash us thoroughly from that iniquity and then we must give that peace permission to come forth by proclaiming *aloud,* so the enemy can hear you, that your trust is in Jesus and in Him alone!

The more we study the Word, the more we trust. The more we trust the more freely the fruit of peace will come forth. Remember 2 Corinthians 1:20 *for all the promises of God in him are yea, and in him amen unto the glory of God by us.* The more we know Him, Christ, the more we will trust Him, and we get to know Him by knowing His Word. Think about this; Do we trust someone freely that we do not know? No, we do not. It goes against every grain of our being. That is why we study, memorize Scripture, and go to church, to get to know Him more. As I said at the beginning Peace is something we seek, crave and at times are desperate for it, now we know what we must do to bear that fruit in our lives. Now it is up to you what you will do with this information.

Homework: **Meditate on John 14:27**

My areas, as God has revealed them, where I am not trusting Him:

_____

_____

_____

_____

_____

My Prayer of repentance from dis-trust:

_____

_____

_____

_____

_____

_____

_____

_____

_____

_____

_____

_____

_____

_____

Do not forget to make your proclamations of trust _aloud_, but also write it down here so you may come back to read it from time to time. That will help you to continue in that trust by recalling what you said to the Lord.

Find in *your* Bible a Scripture that goes with your areas of dis-trust that He revealed to you on the previous page.

For example:

Worry------ Philippians 4:6-7 " Be careful for nothing but in everything by prayer and supplication with thanksgiving let your requests known to God . And the peace of God which passes all understanding will guard your hearts and minds through Christ Jesus."

Area of dis-trust   **Scripture**

_____   _____

                                                    _____

                                                    _____

                                                    _____

Area of dis-trust   **Scripture**

_____   _____

                                                    _____

                                                    _____

                                                    _____

Area of dis-trust   **Scripture**

_____   _____

                                                    _____

                                                    _____

                                                    _____

You have the basic idea now. If you have more than 3 areas continue on notebook paper.

What is your favorite "PEACE" Scripture from page 24? Write it here for 5 days.

_____

_____

_____

_____

_____

_____

_____

_____

_____

_____

_____

_____

_____

_____

_____

_____

_____

_____

_____

_____

_____

_____

_____

What will you do different now when you find that you do not have peace about something?

_____

_____

_____

_____

_____

_____

_____

What do you find different about the PEACE lesson as compared to the others? (The avenue by which we gain the fruit)

_____

_____

_____

_____

_____

_____

_____

_____

_____

_____

_____

_____

PATIENCE

Well here we are at the dreaded fruit of patience. I hope that by now we have gotten rid of all those wrong mind sets and ways of thinking. We do NOT have the ability to "muster up" patience from ourselves, by way of self-will or determination. It is a fruit of the Holy Spirit and comes from Him and Him alone. Because we have the Holy Spirit......we already have patience. Once again I have been intently seeking the Lord as to why we struggle so hard with this particular topic. BUT before I go there I want to share with you something that the Spirit spoke into my heart and encourage me with as I was under attack. Satan does not want the truth of patience to be made known to you however, that precious still small voice spoke to me this, "Every time you overcome, you are advancing the Kingdom of God"! Hallelujah once again ladies we see it is not about us even when we overcome in our personal walk. When we overcome and are free to be all we are to be He can use us to advance His Kingdom and to bring that same "Overcoming Power" to someone else. As hard as some of this is, push through and let the Holy Spirit go to those places in your soul that we have kept for ourselves, that we have hidden from Him (so we think). Let the light of the Word expose you, that truth may raise you up to a fresh and powerful place with God.

I have said all of that to tell you this. Our hindrance, our problem as revealed to me through the Scriptures is contentment. We are not content with things we cannot control. We are not content enough in God to wait. We are not content with where we are in process or the season we are in therefore, we are constantly impatient. We are even discontented with where other people are in the process of sanctification and we deal with them in the attitude of impatience. Oh my Lord, help us I pray. Once again we are going to let the Word of God be our mirror. In Hebrews 4:12 it states-" *For the word of God is quick, and powerful, and sharper than any two edged sword, piercing even to the dividing asunder of soul and spirit, and of the joints and marrow, and is a discerner of the thoughts and intents of the heart."* My desire for you is that the Word of God will set you free and bring to the surface all the areas where you have not been content and then show you how to be content. That is application ladies not merely information!

Long Suffering

Please read carefully the following Verses

Ecclesiastes 7:8
Better is the end of a thing than the beginning thereof; and the **patient** in spirit is better than the proud in spirit.

Luke 8:15
But that on the good ground are they which in an honest and good heart, having heard the Word, keep it, and bring forth fruit with **patience**.

Luke 21:19
In your **patience** possess ye your souls.

JAMES 1:4
BUT LET **PATIENCE** HAVE HER PERFECT WORK, THAT YE MAY BE PERFECT AND ENTIRE LACKING NOTHING.

Hebrews 12:1
Wherefore seeing we also are compassed about with so great a cloud of witnesses, let us lay aside every weight and sin which doth so easily beset us, and let us run with ***patience*** *the race that is set before us.*

James 5:7, 8, 11
[7]Be patient therefore, brethren, unto the coming of the Lord. Behold, the husbandman waiteth for the precious fruit of the earth, and hath long <u>patience</u> for it, until he receive the early and latter rain.
[8]Be ye also <u>patient</u>; stablish your hearts: for the coming of the Lord draweth nigh.

Psalm 37:7
Rest in the Lord, and wait <u>patiently</u> for him; fret not thyself because of him who prospereth in his way, because of the man who bringeth wicked devices to pass.

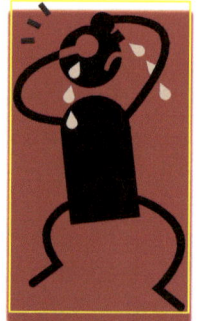

Over and over again as I read those Scriptures I see that *contentment* is the way to **patience**. I see discontentment the hindrance to that fruit working mightily in our lives. We must first recognize that we need patience. Sometimes we do not even know when we are being impatient with **ourselves,** with **others** and yes even **God.** I think if we can see the lack of contentment we will see the impatience. It is very clear to me the two go hand in hand in our lives. One very big problem we have with contentment and patience is we must give up control and trust that God is sovereign and He is in control. God does not need us to help Him control things, situations or people. That my friend is when we get in the way and find ourselves in a place of impatience and discontent full of frustration and anxiety.

We have to give up all control to God, knowing He loves us with an everlasting love and will care for us like no other can. We also have to be content with who we are and where we are with God. We are to always strive to be better, to grow and to learn, however if discontentment is what drives us we will always be impatient trying to achieve some new spiritual level. We will find ourselves unhappy with the "journey" and always feeling like you're not good enough and that is not truth! Look at that verse in Hebrews 12:1...it says to run with patience the race that is set before us. I do not know about you but I have never seen a race that was run patiently. Every race I ever saw the runners were frantic and pushing themselves as hard as they could to reach the finish line to obtain the prize. But our race is not like that. We already have the prize of eternal life so what are we running for? What is our race all about? Well , our race is not about us. Yes here it is again, say, "It's not about me" Our race is for souls.

The souls that without the Word, without our testimony, without our preaching, would otherwise die and spend an eternity in hell. Our race is to take as many people with us to Heaven as we can. Our race is also about loving others on the way, helping them run the race. I think that God wants us to think about it as a race so we will see that we are never to stop but to keep pressing on as we would in a race. Our only competition is satan. But the race has been fixed so to speak therefore, we really need not worry too much about him, we win!! Christ finished the race for us. He is the author and finisher of our faith. Hallelujah, are you getting the picture? The Word of God is telling us to run our race with patience, not to get frantic, anxious, or distressed. Be content with where you are in the race and snatch as many out of the fire as you can, as you run! Help those who have fallen down or gotten weary on the way. And most of all DO NOT STOP RUNNING. If you trip or stumble reach out for a helping hand there should be someone close by to help you out, Jesus is always close by!

Let's look now at the word contentment and what it means

Contentment:
feeling or showing satisfaction with one's possessions, status, or situation

Now let's look at some words that mean the same as contentment and words that are the opposite. Ponder on those this week and ask God to show you where you are content and where you are not content.

Synonyms: CONTENT, CONTENTEDNESS, PLEASURE, DELECTATION, DELIGHT, ENJOYMENT, GLADNESS, GRATIFICATION, HAPPINESS, RELISH, SATISFACTION

Antonyms: DISCONTENT, DISCONTENTEDNESS, DISCONTENTMENT, DISPLEASURE, DISSATISFACTION, UNHAPPINESS

Homework: **Meditate on James 1:4**

Areas where I am content:

_____

_____

_____

_____

_____

_____

_____

Areas where I am not content:

_____

_____

_____

_____

_____

Read again the Scriptures on page 30. Explain how the verse shows the link between contentment and patience.

Ecclesiastes 7:8,9

_____

_____

_____

_____

Luke 8:15

_____

_____

_____

_____

Luke 21:19

_____

_____

_____

_____

James 1:4

_____

_____

_____

_____

Hebrews 12:1

_____

_____

_____

1 Timothy 6:6

_____

_____

_____

_____

James 5:7, 8, 11

_____

_____

_____

_____

Psalm 37:7

_____

_____

_____

_____

Now write out a prayer confessing your areas of discontentment and recognize your need for patience in these areas. Proclaim to God and yourself that you are yielding those areas to the Holy Ghost so that the fruit of patience will not be hindered.

_____

_____

_____

_____

_____

_____

_____

_____

_____

_____

_____

_____

_____

_____

Write out the Patience Verse that speaks to you personally. Write Every day for 5 days.

_____

_____

_____

_____

_____

_____

_____

_____

_____

_____

_____

_____

_____

_____

_____

_____

_____

Gentleness or Kindness

Definition of Gentleness

One *Hebrew* word for gentleness is **anah**. It is a root word with a wide range of meanings: "to *humble* and *abase* oneself in order to *pay attention* to and *respond* to others, to *condescend*, to look down, to keep an eye on, to listen, to sing, to cry out for, to testify, to lift up." *Gentleness is looking past the hardness of a face and seeing a delicate spirit on the inside.*

The Greek word Paul used in the New Testament to describe "gentleness" is the word "prau<thta" (prahotata) from the root Greek word "prau<thj" (prahotes) and it means "*gentleness,*" "*mildness, meekness,*" and there is an aspect of humility in it.

Gentleness is shown in our responses to others, especially those who are under our care. We are to discipline ourselves in order to recognize the weaknesses and limitations of others and respond to them with a soft answer and patient encouragement. We are to nurture them with, wise answers, crying out to God on their behalf, and lifting them up when they falter.

As always I asked the Lord, why we fail here at times and He brought me once again to 1 Thessalonians 2:7. I read it and pondered it, looked it up in a different version and then it came to me. *1Thessolanians 2:7 But we proved to be gentle among you, as a nursing mother tenderly cares for her own children.* In this version (NASB) we can see that the metaphor of gentleness is as a nursing mother tenderly cares for her own children. Therefore what God's Word is telling us is this, "We are to treat people with the same loving, tender, gentle care that a nursing mother would use in caring for her baby" Wow, how I seriously fail at this one. My personality is not naturally gentle, BUT the Holy Spirit can still exhibit that fruit in my life if I just yield and see the need for gentleness. I think that is the key, seeing the need for it. Why should we be gentle? What does it do for others, for us and for the Kingdom? Those are the questions I posed to God and He so graciously answered me.

What does the fruit of Gentleness do for others?

Before we can see what it does we must fix our perspective of people to be the same as God's. I keep hearing the Holy Spirit telling me value people. Therefore the teacher in me wants to make sure we get this right so let's look at what the word "value" *really* means!

Definition of Value:

to consider with respect to worth, excellence, usefulness, or importance.
to regard or esteem highly

According to this definition we are to respect the worth, excellence, usefulness, and importance of others. We are to regard and esteem them highly. My heart began to break as I reflect back on how I have treated others and how it must truly grieve the heart of God and the Holy Spirit in me. We can see that the value of each person is measured by ONE verse in the Bible. John 3:16 *For God so loved the world, that he gave his only begotten Son, that whosoever believeth in him should not perish, but have everlasting life.* Not one person is left out of that. He loves the whole world. He valued all of humanity so He gave His only begotten Son.

What right do we have in judging whether a person deserves to be handled with gentleness? We do not because not one of us deserves it, it is the Love of God that makes us worthy and His love alone. Furthermore as we value people as a mother does her nursing baby, we are allowing the fruit of Gentleness to flow from us and as this happens, that person can tell that you value them and it builds them up and edifies them. If a person is treated with value and Gentleness, it will lift their head and raise them up out of the snare or shame that is holding them back. It annihilates the lie that so often satan tells us, we are not good enough.

This brings me to the verse in Romans 5:8 *But God commendeth his love toward **us**, in that, while we were yet sinners, **Christ died for us**.* He valued us even before we believed in Him, so we too must value others. When we love them with that sense of value then the fruit of gentleness comes forth and can change that person's perspective about themselves. This fruit is very powerful in changing other people's lives as we minister to the body of Christ and as we witness to the lost.

What does the fruit of Gentleness do for us?

That brings me to another verse that is so very powerful. 2 Samuel 22:36 *Thou hast also given me the shield of thy salvation and thy Gentleness hath made me great.* WOW! His Gentleness has made me great! Typically we would think of His power or strength making us great, but here David is proclaiming that it is God's gentleness that has made him great. This verse is part of a song that rose up from David because God had delivered him out of the hands of Saul and all of his enemies. David the mighty warrior KING, Ancestor of Jesus was made great because of Gentleness. So what does the fruit of Gentleness do for us, it makes us great as others observe and see how we treat others, how we value everyone the same no matter where they are; lost, saved, in bondage, or mature in Christ.

What a great testimony for the Lord at work in our lives for others to see that gentleness extended toward someone that the world has cast out or dis- valued. Did not our Lord do the same thing when He went to Zacchaeus' house for supper? It says in Luke 19 that Zacchaeus was the chief among the publicans (tax collector) and was rich. Now Zacchaeus was not someone that people liked very much. But Jesus reached out to him. Read it for yourself. I will be asking questions about this later.

What does the fruit of Gentleness do for the Kingdom or ministry?

This one is easy. We represent the ministry to all those we come into contact with. We represent Christ, His Church, His Kingdom. Read 2Corinthians 6:1, 3-10. All that we do our responses to others, and how we handle those that we are teaching, discipling and ministering to must be in such a way that it testifies of Christ. The way we handle others draws people into the Kingdom and not away. 2 Timothy 2:24 says, *"And the servant of the Lord must not strive; but be gentle unto all men, apt to teach patient."* Titus 3:2 says,*"To speak evil of no man, to be no brawlers, but gentle shewing all meekness unto men."*

Once again we are called to do the impossible that is to be gentle! Once again it is yielding oneself over to the Holy Spirit so that gentleness can come forth. It begins with us valuing others as Christ did when He died for them. The fruit of Gentleness will come from a heart that is not driven by selfishness, self-centered thinking, and does not judge a person by their sin or weakness, but simply reaches out to them with the Love of Christ that says," you were worth it. You were worth the death of the cross!" Gentleness does not decide who is "worthy of gentleness" because it sees everyone the same. A heart of Gentleness does not have a regard for self, but puts others first and esteem them highly. This is only possible for us because of the Holy Spirit living in us. We can be gentle and see the value of others as we should.

Homework: **Meditate on 2 Timothy 2:24**

Write this verse below in the version you are studying

_____

_____

_____

_____

_____

_____

Answer the following questions: YES or NO

Have you developed self-discipline in order to be attentive to the hurts and needs of others?_____

Is your day mostly spent on your own agenda and the meeting of your own needs or the needs of your household?_____

Are you irritable when people with needs intrude upon your time and energy?_____

Do you speak negatively about someone you do not like?_____

Do you look for ways to teach those who are not spiritually mature as they should be?____

Do you give a soft answer so that you do not offend or discourage others?_____

Do you see potential in others and purpose to help them grow in the Lord?_____

When you give instructions or responses to others, do you take into consideration their weakness and limitations?_____

Write out a prayer below asking the Holy Spirit to help you in any of the areas from these questions in which you need help.

_____

_____

_____

_____

_____

_____

_____

_____

_____

_____

In the following Scriptures show how respecting the value of others being the key to the fruit of Gentleness:

2 Timothy 2:24

_____

_____

_____

_____

_____

_____

Titus 3:2

_____

_____

_____

_____

_____

_____

_____

1 Thessalonians 2:7

_____

_____

_____

_____

_____

_____

_____

James3:17

_____

_____

_____

_____

_____

Write out here in your own words why and how we should value others

_____

_____

_____

_____

_____

_____

_____

_____

_____

_____

_____

_____

_____

_____

_____

_____

_____

_____

_____

_____

_____

_____

_____

_____

_____

_____

According to Luke 19: 1-10 the story of Zacchaeus; how did Jesus bear the fruit of gentleness and/or kindness, to show that He valued Zacchaeus and what was the result from that?

_____

_____

_____

_____

_____

_____

_____

_____

_____

_____

_____

_____

_____

GOODNESS

The journey for the revelation on the fruit of *GOODNESS* was different than any of the other fruit. I had to press in and push through to get what God wanted to show me about this fruit. As always my pursuit for understanding began in the Word of God and more specifically in the following Scriptures. **Look them up!**

Psalm 34:8

Psalm 52:1

Psalm 107:8

Psalm118:1

Psalm 119:68

Exodus 34:6

Ezra 3:11

Romans 7:18

Luke 18:19

Matthew 19:17

Romans 2:4

Philippians 4:8

Ephesians 5:8-10

Goodness is the opposite of evil

Goodness is only found in GOD and in His Spirit

JESUS was the living example of GOODNESS

and

Greater works we will do because He goes to the FATHER!

Yes We Can Be Good

Now let's look at some definitions:
Good—*noun* (person, place or thing) that which is morally right or righteous. As an adjective (describes a noun) to be desired or approved
Ness—*suffix* The state of or condition of being something

According to these definitions GOODNESS means the state or condition of being morally right or righteous: it is desired and approved of BUT even Jesus said there was and is only one that is good and that is GOD! (Luke 18:19, Matt 19:17) *So where does that leave us?*

We will get to that in just a little bit. I don't know about you but after reading those very academic definitions of GOOD and GOODNESS I was still left without a clear picture of what it all *really* meant. I knew it was more, its meaning deeper. So I looked up the opposite of good or its antonyms and then I began to understand. It seems to be more clearly defined by what it is *not*. GOOD is not- bad, evil, unholy, ungodly, unrighteous, unloving, unkind, etc...

Look once again at Philippians 4:8 Here is a very clear list of what is good!

Finally, brethren, whatsoever things are true, whatsoever things are honest, whatsoever things are just, whatsoever things are pure, whatsoever things are lovely, whatsoever things are of good report; if there be any virtue, and if there be any praise, think on these things.

Now to go back to the previous problem; if even Jesus said only God is good where does that leave us? Based on the Scriptures it is obvious that GOODNESS is part of the very essence of God. He is GOOD. He does not just do good things like we do sometimes. He does not merely exhibit good behavior or good attributes. He *is* GOODNESS. Everything He creates is GOOD Because He *is* GOODNESS. He cannot be contrary to what He is therefore everything He does *is* GOOD. Once again where does that leave us in relation to bearing the fruit of goodness? I have come to this very simple yet complex conclusion. In order to show forth the fruit of GOODNESS we must be completely yielded over to the Holy Spirit and our flesh cannot be ruling us. This fruit will manifest from a vessel that is living for Kingdom purposes bringing their natural man under subjection to the spirit man constantly. The fruit of GOODNESS is Pure, Holy, and undefiled by sin, evil and the fallen nature of man. The fruit of GOODNESS is a manifestation of the very presence of a Holy God. I know this sounds like it is impossible, but it is not or He would not have put it in His Word. I believe it begins with Philippians 4:8 and doing what it says. I know you have heard it said "garbage in...garbage out" And we can stand on what Romans 12:1-2 says (look it up in your Bible) We must be constantly renewing our minds with truth and proclaiming to our fleshly bodies that it is the temple of the Holy Ghost, 1 Corinthians 6:19 (look it up). When we are walking in GOODNESS , bearing that fruit, we bring the very part of Him that turns dark into light, overcomes evil and sends every demon running. You do not have to speak a word, just yield to His Spirit in your life in all the areas that He is asking you for. He alone knows those areas that you have yet to give Him. Will you dare to become the kind of disciple that lives for Him and not yourself in any way? Do you dare to become the kind of warrior that all you have to do is show up and the darkness has to flee, because evil cannot remain when the GOODNESS of GOD has arrived?

Homework: **Meditate on Philippians 4:8**

Read the following and answer the questions

Romans 6:12-14
Let not sin therefore reign in your mortal body, that ye should obey it in the lusts thereof.
Neither yield ye your members as instruments of unrighteousness unto sin: but yield yourselves unto God, as those that are alive from the dead, and your members as instruments of righteousness unto God.
For sin shall not have dominion over you: for ye are not under the law, but under grace.

Explain what this verse is telling us and how is it important as pertaining to bearing the fruit of the Spirit.

_____

_____

_____

_____

_____

_____

_____

_____

_____

_____

_____

_____

_____

_____

Read Matthew 17:15-21. Why do you think the disciples could not cast out the demon? What does fasting and prayer have to do with it and how does that relate to what we have learned about the fruit of GOODNESS?

_____

_____

_____

_____

_____

_____

_____

_____

_____

_____

_____

_____

_____

_____

_____

_____

_____

_____

_____

_____

_____

Read Romans 12:21- Explain how we overcome evil with good based on what we have learned about "Goodness" and what does the "Goodness" of God do to the works of darkness?

_____

_____

_____

_____

_____

_____

_____

_____

_____

_____

_____

_____

_____

_____

_____

_____

_____

_____

_____

_____

_____

_____

What type of situations do you think would call for the fruit of GOODNESS and what would the result be?

_____

_____

_____

_____

_____

_____

_____

_____

Psalm 23 :6 states "Surely **goodness** and mercy shall follow me all the days of my life and I will dwell in the house of the Lord forever." What does that mean to you personally reflecting on how we have defined goodness.

_____

_____

_____

_____

_____

_____

_____

_____

_____

Faithfulness

Faithfulness—as used in the context of the fruit of the Spirit in Galatians 5 means, *the character of one who can be relied on*

This definition did surprise me. I was so sure that this lesson would be all about having faith and believing God; however from my digging, studying and asking for the Holy Ghost to reveal the understanding to me, I found that it is only part of what this lesson is about. Let's look at more words that refer to the character of one who can be relied upon and get the picture.

Committed—bound or obligated, as under a pledge to a particular cause, action, or attitude;

Dependable—worthy of reliance or trust; worthy of trust or belief; consistent in performance or behavior

Steadfast—Fixed or unchanging; steady; firmly loyal or constant; unswerving; fixed in intensity or direction; steady; unwavering or determined in purpose, loyalty; marked by firm determination or resolution; not shakable

All of those words are synonyms of Faithfulness in the context of the fruit. As I read those definitions I began to see the full measure of what faithfulness really means. Faithfulness sees things through to the end. It has a resolve that says, "I am not moving, I am committed to this and will stand firm on my convictions." Faithfulness is not moved by the world or the circumstances of this life. Faithfulness can stay committed, dependable and steadfast because its focus is on God and His faithfulness. A person who has the *true* fruit of faithfulness abounding in their life is driven by their faith and trust in Christ and *His* faithfulness. I am beginning to see that a person can be committed, dependable, and steadfast but not walking in the fruit of faithfulness. How do I know that? Well, let me ask you this, How many committed, dependable, and steadfast people do you know that have no joy in their life, no peace, have control issues, complain about what others are not doing, complain about what they are doing.....I could go on and on with that list. That my friend is not a person who is abounding in the fruit of faithfulness, they are driven by obligation and have gotten their eyes off of why they are doing what they are doing. The force that drives them is the need, or doing for a person, or for their own self-fulfillment, or they have control issues, or they just cannot see something *not* get done! Also there is one more dangerous place we can go that is taking on *false responsibility.* That is taking on things that God never intended you to take on, but you missed Him telling you not to do it because His voice gets so crowed out with all those other driving forces.

When He alone is our driving force we have clear instructions on what we are to do and not to do. We cannot be moved to action because of needs. We must be moved only by the Holy Spirit. I am just listing things as God brings them to me. If you find yourself in ANY of these problem areas then you must begin praying now and ask God to help you see how to get your perspective back to what it needs to be; and that is, it's all about Jesus!

It is our faith and belief in Jesus Christ and what He completed on the cross for you that is/and /or should be our driving force that keeps us in the character of faithfulness. It should **never**, **ever** be servant hood to obligations or mere commitments to a task, job, position or person.

Keeping our commitments and being accountable is part of being a faithful servant. That is why we must hear and know what God wants us to do so we have that "stick-to-it-ness" When we have that Word from God and the *desire* and *unction* from the Holy Spirit is there equipping us we are committed, dependable and steadfast in the work of the Kingdom. No demon in hell will keep us from our post. That is when the fruit of faithfulness abounds in our life and we have true joy and fulfillment as we serve even in the small menial tasks. Just remember it may appear to others that we are faithful because we are working, and serving, but in reality we are weary, frustrated and in bondage.

Does this mean we need to stop what we are doing? Maybe, but it does mean we have lost hold somehow on what our true reason for serving should be. Ask the Holy Spirit to search your heart and let the Word of God lead you to a correct perspective. Let the Word encourage you with the faithfulness of God. You will see that we can be faithful because He is so faithful to us! In the home work you will read many verses about God's faithfulness and about how we are to be faithful. Let the Word of God speak to your heart and show you His standard of faithfulness. You will see that it is a very high standard.

Once again ladies remember as we learn, we yield those areas over to Him and as we do that, we become strong in that area because it is HIM that is doing it. Hallelujah!

Homework: **Meditate on Hebrews 10:23**

Read the following Verses in your Bible. Determine which ones are referring to His faithfulness and which ones are referring to our faithfulness. Choose your favorite in both categories and be ready to share with the group what they mean to you.

2Timothy 2:13   **Matthew 25:14-30**   **1Corinthians 15:58**
1 Thessalonians 5:24   **Colossians 3:22**   **Luke 16:10**
Psalms 36:5   **Psalms 119:75**   **Luke 19:11-27**
1 Corinthians 1:9   **2 Thessalonians 3:3**   **Matthew 5:37**
James 5:12   **Lamentations 3:23**   **Hebrews 10:23**

Faithfulness of God   Our Faithfulness

_____   _____

_____   _____

_____   _____

_____   _____

_____   _____

_____   _____

_____   _____

_____   _____

_____   _____

_____   _____

_____   _____

_____   _____

_____   _____

_____   _____

What have you learned about your own motives for commitment or serving and what do you need to do differently? **Put a Scripture with your answer.**

_____

_____

_____

_____

_____

_____

_____

How does a person get their perspective on the wrong thing concerning faithfulness and being committed?

_____

_____

_____

_____

_____

_____

_____

_____

_____

_____

_____

_____

_____

According to the Scriptures you have read what are some ways that God is faithful to us?

_____

_____

_____

_____

_____

_____

_____

_____

How does knowing God's faithfulness to us encourage our faithfulness to Him?

_____

_____

_____

_____

_____

_____

_____

_____

_____

_____

_____

_____

What do you think will happen to a person if they spend their time being pulled and moved by needs, people or obligations and they never correct their perspective or motive?

_____

_____

_____

_____

_____

_____

_____

_____

Write out a prayer here telling the Lord that you are committed to Him and Him alone. Ask Him to keep your focus solely on Him and your motive be true to serving Him even as you serve others.

_____

_____

_____

_____

_____

_____

_____

_____

Meekness

Definition—In an evangelical sense; humility; resignation; submission to the devine will, without murmuring; opposed to pride, arrogance.

Think on these statements:

Meekness is a grace which Jesus alone exemplified and which no ancient philosopher seems to have understood or recommended *(Noah Webster's 1913 On-line Dictionary)*

Meekness is a spiritual temperament that says, "YES" to God in *joyful* obedience. It is slow to *give* or *take* offense. It is *teachable* and rests upon the grace of humility.
(Prayers that Prevail)

Look at these words that mean the opposite of meekness:

Arrogant, conceited, egotistic, haughty, high-and-mighty, presuming, self-asserting, superior, prideful, self-centered, cocky, self- engrossed, overbearing, patronizing, dominant, condescending

*If you do not know the meaning of all of these words or statements, look them up. It is **very** important that you fully understand what meekness is NOT!*

I know I am giving you a lot of information, however as I researched this fruit one common theme kept rising to the surface. Let's look now at the Word of God and I will explain to you what this theme is.

Ephesians 4:1-2
I therefore, the prisoner of the Lord, beseech you that ye walk worthy of the vocation wherewith ye are called, with all lowliness and meekness, with longsuffering, forbearing one another in love.

Can you walk this type of walk in your "self"?_____ Yes or No

1 Timothy 6:11-12
11But thou, O man of God, flee these things; and follow after righteousness, godliness, faith, love, patience, meekness.
12Fight the good fight of faith, lay hold on eternal life, whereunto thou art also called, and hast professed a good profession before many witnesses.

Can you walk this type of walk in your "self"? _____ Yes or No

Colossians 3:12
Put on therefore, as the elect of God, holy and beloved, bowels of mercies, kindness, humbleness of mind, meekness, longsuffering.

Can you walk this type of walk in your "self"? _____ Yes or No

1 Peter 2:20
For what credit is there if, when you sin and are harshly treated, you endure it with patience? But if when you do what is *right* and suffer *for it* you patiently endure it, *this* finds favor with God.

Can you walk this type of walk in your "self"? _____ Yes or No

Based on all the definitions and Verses that the Holy Spirit took me, I see very clearly this fact:

MEEKNESS DEMANDS THAT "SELF" BE DEAD

Now let's look at some Biblical examples that God has put in His Word for us to follow. Look up the following verses.

Moses—Numbers 12:3- Moses submitted to the will of God with great meekness; Giving of his own life to be the deliverer of the people.

David—1 Samuel 24 Read the whole chapter. David did not strive with Saul.

Jeremiah—Jeremiah 26:12-15 obeyed God, he did not strive with his enemy but trusted God.

Stephen—Acts 7: 54-60 Stephen prayed for those that were killing him.

Paul—2 Timothy 4:13-18, Paul stated that it not be laid to their charge for opposing his ministry of the Gospel.

Jesus—Isaiah 53:7, Jesus never opened His mouth in protest or in His own defense. He yielded to the Father's will all the way to the cross.

Our natural man will never be able to bear the fruit of meekness. It goes against the very nature of our humanity that wants to have its say, or defend itself, or be offended, or claim its rights. You have the picture. God tells us over and over in His Word that we are to exhibit meekness, walk in meekness, however as we read what His Word is saying, it seems impossible to do! The only way we can truly be meek is by our spirit man who is governed ONLY by the Holy Spirit. If we are not praying, not spending time in the Word, not praising Him, not gathering with other believers, we will become spiritually weak. Our natural man will be the stronger. BUT when we yield to the Holy Spirit in us, spend time in the Word, spend time praising the Lord, Spend time with other believers being edified by the body of Christ, our spirit man is strong, very strong. Just as we have been learning all throughout these lessons it begins with yielding.

We cannot learn to bear the fruit BUT we can learn to yield to the Spirit in us so the fruit can come forth. We have all we need because of the indwelling power of the Holy Spirit, however, we can be doing all the right things, BUT if we do not *yield* to the Holy Spirit the fruit just simply will not come forth. For some reason it is very hard for us to let go of that natural part of us, however if we want the power of meekness, we must! Meekness is a powerful fruit, it was that character that came forth when Christ was battling in the garden (Matthew 26:36-46) before He was to go to the cross. Meekness ministered to the Thief (Luke 23:43) hanging next to Him for Christ was not consumed with His own pain. Also, let us be quick to remember Christ also cried (Luke 23:34) out on behalf of His enemy as He was about to die, asking God to forgive them for they know not what they do. There are many more times that Christ showed forth meekness.

Meekness is shown through Christ in such a way that we can clearly see He was not submitted to the natural part of Him, but He was totally yielded to the God part of Him. What a beautiful thing! Now we must be quick to say "Greater Works We Will Do....!" God is calling us to be meek knowing full well that it will have to be His Spirit in us, keeping us pressing in to Him, pushing through all of ourselves in order to bear that powerful fruit to glorify Him and change the lives of others.

Remember the fruit is not for us, it is for others. It is the power of God flowing through us to change the atmosphere around us, sending every demon fleeing from our presence, or to change someone's life. The fruit of meekness is the ministry of Christ. Meekness does not defend itself when treated wrong because it sees the bigger picture. Now let me say this, it is crucial that we are lead by the Spirit and know that God is calling us to a place of meekness in a situation, because sometimes He is calling us to take a stand and say "NO" to how we are being treated. It is vital that you be yielded and lead by the Lord so that you are not remaining in an abusive situation. We must hear God on the matter, always!

Homework:　　　**Meditate on Isaiah 53:7**

Since Jesus' ministry is the perfect example of meekness, your assignment is to find 3 examples in the Gospels (*the books of Matthew, Mark, Luke and John*) where Jesus exhibited meekness. Give the Scripture reference and your explanation on how it is the example of meekness.

Example #1

_____

_____

_____

_____

_____

_____

_____

_____

_____

Example #2

_____

_____

_____

_____

_____

_____

_____

_____

_____

Example #3

_____
_____
_____
_____
_____
_____
_____
_____
_____
_____

What are some ways that we must die to "self" in order for the fruit of meekness to come forth in our lives.

_____
_____
_____
_____
_____
_____
_____
_____

How can exhibiting the fruit of meekness in your life change the life of someone else?

_____

_____

_____

_____

_____

_____

_____

_____

_____

_____

Find in your Bible 2 "dying to self" or "crucifying self" Verses. Write them out here.
(If you find more than 2 that's great!)

_____

_____

_____

_____

_____

_____

_____

_____

_____

_____

_____

_____

_____

_____

_____

_____

_____

_____

_____

_____

_____

_____

_____

Now, using the Verses you have written on the previous page write out a prayer personalizing those verses and proclaiming to your Lord that you are submitting to "dying to self" or "crucifying the flesh" in order for the fruit of meekness to flow freely from your life to change the world around you!

_____

_____

_____

_____

_____

_____

_____

_____AMEN!

TEMPERANCE
Self-Control

TEMPERANCE—Moderation; particularly, habitual moderation in regard to the indulgence of the natural appetites and passions; restrained or moderate indulgence; as temperance in eating and drinking; temperance in the indulgence of joy or mirth. Temperance in eating and drinking is opposed to gluttony and drunkenness, and in other indulgences, to excess.

SELF-CONTROL
The ability to exercise restraint or control over one's feelings, emotions, reactions, etc.

The act of denying yourself; controlling your impulses

Look up the following passages of Scripture and let's see what the Word of God is telling us about temperance and self-control:

2 Peter 1:3-8   Titus 1:7-9   Proverbs 25:28
1 Corinthians 9:24-27   Proverbs 16:32

Once again we find ourselves between a rock and a hard place. God calls us to be temperate, yet self cannot control self. Self is our problem. When self is running things that's when it turns bad. So what is God telling us? We must yield over "self" to the control of the Holy Spirit. How do I know this? I know this because, if we could accomplish the type of balanced temperance and self-control that the Word of God describes, then we would not need HIM. When we got saved and signed on to serve God and made Jesus our Lord, then He says to us, "Let Me do ALL the things in you that you will never be able to accomplish on your own!" Temperance is a big one because it covers such a broad scope of issues in our life.

Let's look at some of them; anger, appetites, passions, desires. Some of the ways that we get out of control is in the flesh or areas that directly relate to our bodies. And other ways are pertaining to our emotions and our will.

The *lack* of self-control affects our whole being as well as, the *presence* of self-control also affects our whole being. When we make Jesus our Lord and we choose to be His bond slave, we step into an unlimited benefit program. This means if He is truly Lord and we yield over self to Him, He has free reign to control our responses, appetites, passions, desires and all the areas where we typically step out of balance. Hallelujah!! Our job is to look at ourselves with truth and humility and find the areas where we are over indulgent or out of control and purposefully begin to yield that area to Him. He will gladly take it. Let me make this statement; He wants to control those areas not to take anything away from us BUT to free us from the consequences of our out of control actions; to free us from the torment of regret, shame and guilt. His Lording over us is something He desires to do *for* us not as a man would lord over us, but as a loving and merciful God who knows we would be a mess without His grace and strength in our lives. Thank You Jesus!

We need not be fearful in giving up control to Him because we know from His Word that He wants **GOOD** things for His children.(Jeremiah 29:11) As we grow more and more in this principle of yielding control of ourselves to Him we will see who we are in Christ with our unique personalities and gifts. We will begin to see HIM in areas of our life where we did not like ourselves. I remember writing in my journal one day a long time ago; I said "I like myself when it is Christ that I see". We gain who we truly are created to be when we lose ourselves in Him. (Matthew 10:39) We are all a new creature in Christ Jesus when we are born again but it takes this yielding of self for it to manifest. What freedom it brings to my heart when I think on the fact that I cannot do it BUT He can and wants to do it for me. We are truly crazy if we choose to stay in control ourselves, don't you think? So why do we hang on to controlling ourselves? That my friend is an individual answer, different for each of us, but a question we do need to ask ourselves. And in that answer is your starting place for yielding all control over to Him. Read the scriptures over and over until the Holy Spirit reveals to you why you are hanging on to control. Ask Him to search you and bring to your mind and heart what your true reason is.

Also, consider this, as we grow in this yielding over self process, we will bear more and more of ALL the fruit of the Spirit, because is not self truly our main hindrance? Even if we label it dis-trust, discontentment, pride, disobedience, dis-valuing people, wrong motives, being bad, all of the things that we have discovered that hinder the other fruit of the Spirit, isn't it SELF?? If we look at our journey through these fruit we can clearly see that we started on the surface but with each one we went a little deeper into ourselves as well into the Word, until we ultimately ended up here at self-control. That is no coincidence ladies. Here at temperance and self-control is where the rubber meets the road.

Do you *REALLY* believe everything you have been learning and studying all these weeks? Are you ready to give control to Him, by way of the Holy Spirit in you, and let your life as well as YOU be changed? Is this a onetime thing? NO!! It will become a life style as you put everything to practice that you have learned. We can do this ladies because it is not us that does the work; it is the indwelling power of the Holy Spirit that achieves what we cannot. It is so very fitting that temperance and self-control are the last fruit in the list.

God ordained that order in His Word and now we can take all that He has shown us and turn everything upside down, sending the enemy running from our homes, from our church; anywhere we go, simply by yielding control over to our Lord and allowing the character of Christ to become our character. What do we have to lose from yielding control over to Him? Absolutely nothing worth keeping!

What do we have to gain?
>   Freedom from sin
>   Freedom from regret
>   Freedom from shame and guilt
>   Freedom from lies and all the power that the Holy Spirit possess

However if you choose to still want to *learn* to bear the fruit and you desire to keep control yourself He will let you and be ever so patiently waiting for you to make the choice to give it up and yield to Him.

Which one of the Scriptures listed on the first page of this lesson gives a description of how a Pastor or Bishop should live the example of temperance. Put in your own words the list of "do's and don'ts."

_____

_____

_____

_____

_____

_____

_____

_____

Do you think we should also exhibit those same attributes even though we are not Pastors or

Bishops? _____

If your answer is YES explain why. If your answer is NO explain why.

_____

_____

_____

_____

_____

_____

_____

_____

Read Proverbs 25:28. What do you think it means to "be like a city that is broken down and without walls"?

_____

_____

_____

_____

_____

_____

_____

_____

_____

_____

_____

How does the enemy take advantage of us when we are not yielding control of self to the Holy Spirit?

_____

_____

_____

_____

_____

Which one of the Scriptures on the first page of this lesson talks about the strength of one who exhibits self-control?_____

Explain how it shows that and what does having that type of strength mean to you in your life.

_____

_____

_____

_____

_____

_____

_____

_____

_____

_____

_____

Read 2 Peter 1: 3-4

Does this Scripture show us that we have all we need?_____

What do you think "partakers of the divine nature" means?

_____

_____

_____

_____

How did we escape the corruption that is in the world?

_____

_____

_____

_____

If we give all control to Him do we then lose are uniqueness our personality? Put your answer with a Scripture?

_____
_____
_____
_____
_____
_____
_____
_____
_____
_____

According to 1 Corinthians 9:24-27 we will win a crown, what kind of crown will a yielded

vessel of the Lord win? _____ and why?_____

_____
_____
_____
_____
_____
_____
_____
_____
_____
_____
_____
_____
_____
_____
_____
_____

Answer the questions about the following Scripture:

1 Corinthians 9:27
but I discipline my body and make it my slave, so that, after I have preached to others, I myself will not be disqualified.

How is the verse talking about temperance or self-control?

_____

_____

_____

_____

_____

_____

What do you think Paul meant by, "I myself will not be disqualified?"

_____

_____

_____

_____

Is there an old saying that comes to mind? I will give you a hint. It begins with:

"Practice _____ _____ _____**"**

Seek the Lord about why you hesitate in giving up control to His Spirit in you and write down what He shows you.

_____

_____

_____

_____

_____

_____

_____

_____

_____

Write out a prayer here proclaiming that you have need that He control you and that you are giving it up to Him.

_____

_____

_____

_____

_____

_____

_____

_____

_____

_____

_____

_____

_____

_____

_____

_____

_____

List all the things you can think of that you have to gain by giving ALL control to Him. After each one, write "thank You Lord"

Example: *I will gain freedom from food controlling me. Thank you Lord!*

_____

_____

_____

_____

_____

_____

_____

_____

_____

_____

My Lord, I thank You for all that you have taught us from Your Word, how awesome it has been. May we now keep close at hand all that we have learned about ourselves, about You and Your Word. Lord, remind us when we fall back into wrong mind sets like, "satan can steal our joy" and that we have to "learn to bear the fruit", that we have all we need because of Your Holy Spirit that is alive in us. That the same power that raised Christ from the dead dwells in us. Convict our hearts when we get stubborn and do not yield. Stir your Word in us when we need to be reminded of what it says. Raise us up to a new level with you as we yield over more and more of us to You. We are your ladies my Lord. We do not belong to ourselves; we are your bond slaves who freely give of our hearts, minds, bodies, time, gifts and talents to further Your Kingdom. Thank You for the freedom that comes with the knowledge that it is not about us! Hallelujah! Make us a blessing wherever we go. May we hold our heads up high with bold confidence in who you are and what You have done. Thank you my Lord for your Word and all the ways it has changed us, loved us, convicted us and set us free. We choose to never be the same. We choose to follow after your Word and we choose to yield and let ALL the precious fruit of the Holy Spirit flow freely from our lives. Hallelujah, In Jesus Name!!

Facilitators Guide

This Bible study is designed for groups of variable sizes and can be very flexible in order to meet the group's needs. There must be a leader who has completed the home work for the lesson that is being reviewed and the *new* one that is being introduced. The facilitator must be one who can commit to be at the Bible study for every meeting. The following are helpful pointers that I used in leading the Kamikaze for Christ Bible Study in my community.

Choose a night that is convenient for everyone and do not change it if at all possible. I have found that when we keep the time and day consistent the ones who *really* want to learn and grow, make arrangements to be there. Ours is on Monday nights at 7:00pm

I laid out guidelines for the women so they would know what to expect:

1. We start at 7pm and we will end at 9pm

2. We will discuss the Bible Study, the Word and of course God, if they need counseling that is not the time for it. This is not a women's support group, nor is it prayer request time.

3. Those 2 hours are dedicated to the Lord to teach us and reveal His Word to us. This is not personal testimony time. It is not time for them to talk about themselves unless it pertains to the lesson.

4. I explained to them, if someone takes over talking way to much taking up time needlessly, they will be interrupted and asked that we stay on topic. Now I know what you are thinking, that if you tell them that they will all shut down and never talk or participate, but that is not what happened in our group. I explained to them that we are women and it is in our nature to talk, share and unload on one another, but if we really want what God has for us, we must give Him control and pray that the words that we speak, the questions we ask, the points and perspectives we bring up will be ordained of Him so that we all, will be adding to the richness and depth of the class. It worked wonderfully in our meetings. We learned from each other and it was rich with all the different perspectives that we brought out. God blessed us because we disciplined ourselves. Don't be afraid to be a firm facilitator. Don't micro manage, don't overly control, but in *love*, keep everyone on topic. Be flexible yet structured always allowing God to move things the way He wants. If they are true women of God, they will respect you for it and be thankful, that you are maintaining that in the group.

The Bible study is designed in such a way that the homework is done during the week and when you come to the meeting you are reviewing the homework questions and then receiving the next lesson. In the first meeting you should go over all the guidelines, and that they will be expected to complete homework every week before the next meeting and working on any memorization work. Tell them they will be expected to participate in discussions. I told my ladies that if they did not volunteer to participate, to be ready for me to call on them. I made sure they all felt equally important and that what they had to share was just as good as anyone else's.

Your first meeting may not be a whole 2 hours. However as the facilitator I strongly suggest that you complete the introductory lesson before your first meeting so you can talk about it. Bring up some points that spoke to you, but not so much as you end up reviewing the entire lesson. On the first meeting I always like to ask each person what motivated them to come and what are they hoping to take away from this Bible Study. I always let them know that the responsibility of whether or not this is a good Bible study does not rest upon the facilitator it rest upon them. It will be as good as they make it and according to their commitment. This always makes for good discussion. We sometimes bring up the things we allow to get in the way of Bible Study and together as a group we decide to not allow those things to hinder us. I always get everyone's contact information at the first meeting.

As you hand out the work books, be sure to tell them not to work ahead. It is designed that everyone completes one lesson a week. After the first meeting it is easy. As the facilitator you must always be one lesson ahead of the group so that you can do some kind of introduction into the new lesson. As you work the lessons yourself, make notes as God leads. God knows the needs of your group of women and He will speak to your heart as to what needs extra attention in the lesson.

Most of all pray over the women at the beginning of each meeting. I found that as the women were arriving they were in rush, very tense, stressed out and tired. I would pray for them, that during those 2 hours they would find rest, and a freedom from stress and all that pulls at them. That for those 2 hours they were not mom, wife.....they were simply His child and we are all crawling up in Daddy's lap for a bit a see what He had to say to us.

For a very last meeting I ask everyone to prepare something in order to share what part of the Bible Study ministered to them and in what way did it change them. That is a very special time and it is very touching to see how the Word and the Holy Spirit worked through their own efforts to grow them, touch them, and change them.

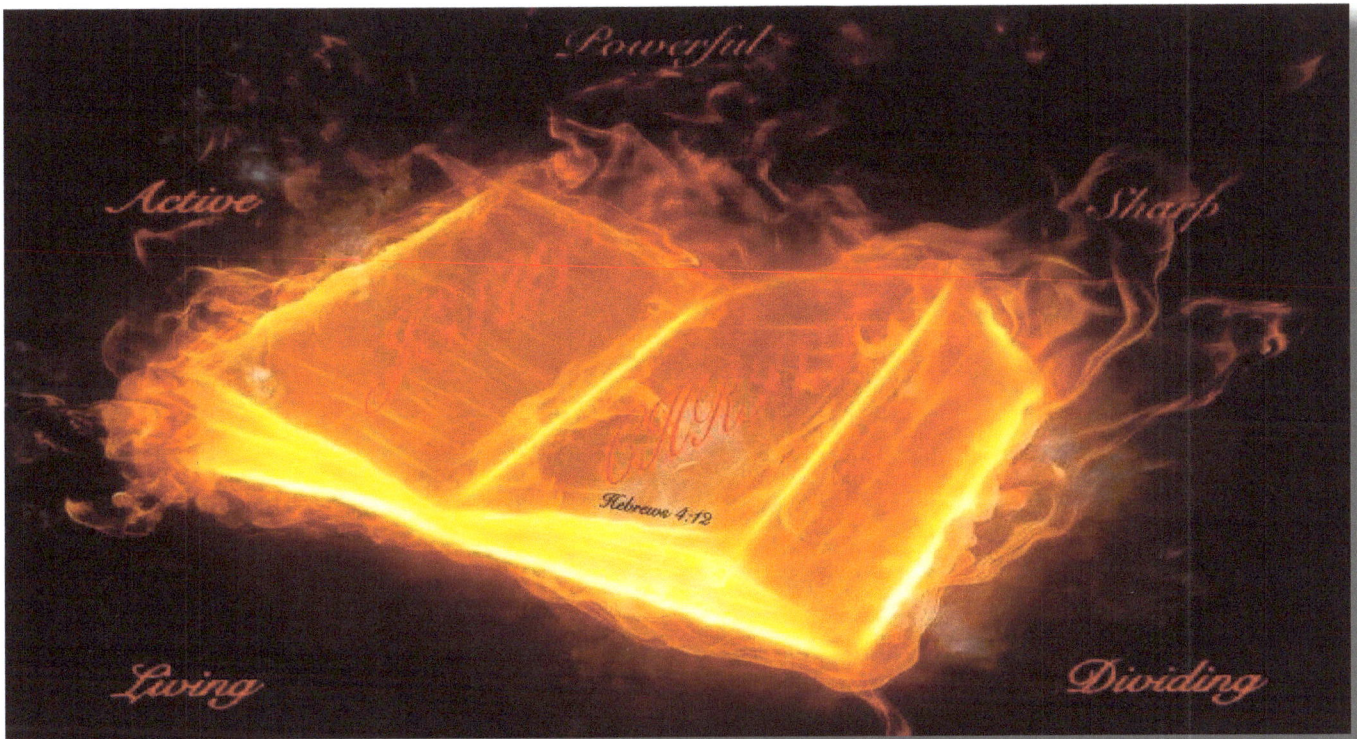

You must allow the Holy Spirit be the guide through you. As the facilitator you set the tone for the meeting therefore keep that in mind as you go throughout your day. I would love to know about your group and how things are going so I can pray for you and if at any time you have any questions about anything in the bible study please send me an e mail with your question. I am confident in the Word of God that it will truly bless you, build you up in faith, and cause you to go a little deeper and closer with God. Peace be unto you and you group. May the very Presence of Jehovah be manifested in and through you. In Jesus Name.

Dana Poole

poolend1@gmail.com

Kamikaze for Christ

To live is Christ; to die is gain.
—Phil 1:21

Memory Verses

Primary Memory Verse: Galatians 5:22-25

Love	Romans 5:5
Joy	John 15:11
Peace	John14:27
Patience/Long Suffering	James 1:4
Gentleness/Kindness	2Timothy 2:24
Goodness	Philippians 4:8
Faithfulness	Hebrews 10:23
Meekness	Isaiah 53:7
Temperance/Self-control	Proverbs 25:28

To get the most out of this Bible study and really experience life changing results, memorize these Verses. It is the Word that renews and transforms our minds. The Word of God will change in you what we cannot change. Be blessed and yield to His Spirit in you, walk in the fullness of His power and change the atmosphere everywhere you go.

Blessings and Peace,
Dana Poole
Kamikaze for Christ

To live is Christ; to die is gain.
Philippians 1:21

www.ingramcontent.com/pod-product-compliance
Lightning Source LLC
Chambersburg PA
CBHW061353090426

42739CB00002B/15

9 780692 383605